A Kid's Guide to Drawing the Countries of the World™

How to Draw
Russia's
Sights and Symbols

Melody S. Mis

The Rosen Publishing Group's
PowerKids Press™
New York

To Gretchen, Kim, and Kelly

Published in 2004 by The Rosen Publishing Group, Inc.
29 East 21st Street, New York, NY 10010

First Edition

Editor: Jannell Khu
Book Design: Kim Sonsky
Layout Design: Michael de Guzman

Illustration Credits: Cover and inside by Emily Muschinske except p. 17 (ruble) by Mike Donnellan.
Photo Credits: Cover and p. 38 © Yogi, inc./CORBIS; p. 4 © Hulton-Deutsch collection/CORBIS; p. 9 © The State Russian Museum/CORBIS; p. 10 © Gianni Dagli Orti/CORBIS; p. 12 © The Bridgeman Art Library International; p. 13 © Scala/Art Resource, NY; p. 18 © Reuters NewMedia Inc./CORBIS; p. 20 © Raymond Gehman/CORBIS; p. 22 © Diego Lezama Orezzoli/CORBIS; p. 24 © Jean-Pierre Lescourret/CORBIS; p. 26 © Brian A. Vikander/CORBIS; p. 28 © Bruce Adams; Eye Ubiquitous/CORBIS; p. 30 © Steve Raymer/CORBIS; p. 32 © Kevin Schafer/CORBIS; p. 34 © Culver Pictures, Inc.; p. 36 © Roger Ressmeyer/CORBIS; p. 40 © Steve Raymer/CORBIS; p. 42 © Corbis Sygma.

Mis, Melody S.
How to draw Russia's sights and symbols / Melody S. Mis.
    p. cm. — (A Kid's guide to drawing the countries of the world)
Summary: Presents step-by-step directions for drawing the national flag, Winter Palace, matryoshka dolls, and other sights and symbols of Russia.

Includes bibliographical references and index.
ISBN 0-8239-6666-6 (library binding)
1. Drawing—Technique—Juvenile literature. 2. Russia (Federation)—In art—Juvenile literature. [1. Russia (Federation)—In art. 2. Drawing—Technique.] I. Title. II. Series.
NC665 .M57 2004
743.83647—dc21

2002153345

Manufactured in the United States of America

CONTENTS

Let's Draw Russia

Slav farmers established the first Russian state by A.D. 800 along the Volga River in western Russia. It was called Kievan Rus. The Slavs were descendants of indigenous peoples from eastern Europe. When Scandinavian Vikings, called Varangian Russes, conquered the Slavs in the mid-800s, they renamed the region the Land of Rus. This was how Russia got its name.

During the thirteenth century, the Mongolian army from Asia, called the Golden Horde, conquered the Land of Rus. They ruled for about 200 years. In the fifteenth century, Ivan III, the grand prince of Moscow, united Russia and established Russia's independence from Mongolia. In 1547, Ivan IV became the first Russian ruler to be called czar. The word "czar" comes from the Russian word for caesar, or a country's highest ruler. In 1613, the Romanov family came into power and ruled Russia for 300 years. The Romanovs brought back order and increased trade with other countries. Peter the Great ruled Russia from 1682 to 1725. He reformed the government, improved

Ivan IV of Russia was called Ivan the Terrible because he burned towns, killed church leaders, and established a serfdom. A serf was someone who was like a slave.

factories, and made Russia a major world power. Some of the rulers to follow Peter were Catherine II, Alexander I, and Alexander II. They continued the reforms, but peasants still did not enjoy full rights. This led to rebellions, workers' strikes, and civil war.

Many peasants joined the Communist Party, begun in 1903 by Vladimir Ilich Lenin. Communism is a system of government that is defined by a classless society and state ownership of all businesses.

After the Bolshevik Revolution of 1917, Lenin and the Communists took control of the government and formed the Union of Soviet Socialist Republics (USSR). Lenin died in 1924, and Joseph Stalin ruled Russia for the next 30 years. At the end of World War II in 1945, Stalin cut off contact with all western countries. The USSR was said to be sealed behind an imaginary wall called the Iron Curtain. This caused a distrust between the East and the West that became known as the cold war and lasted until the 1980s.

During the cold war, Russia fired the first manned spacecraft into space and built the first nuclear satellite. During the 1980s, President Mikhail Gorbachev freed political prisoners, improved relations with the West, and began economic reforms. In 1991, the USSR was split into 12 independent countries. Russia is the largest. Today most of these countries belong to the Commonwealth of Independent States (CIS). This book will teach you how to draw Russia's sights and symbols. You will start with simple shapes and add other shapes to them. Directions are under each drawing, and each new step is shown in red. You will need the following supplies to draw Russia's sights and symbols:

- A sketch pad
- An eraser
- A number 2 pencil
- A pencil sharpener

These are some of the shapes and drawing terms you need to know to draw Russia's sights and symbols:

— Horizontal line

⟿ Squiggle

⬭ Oval

⬜ Trapezoid

▭ Rectangle

△ Triangle

▮ Shading

| Vertical line

∿ Wavy line

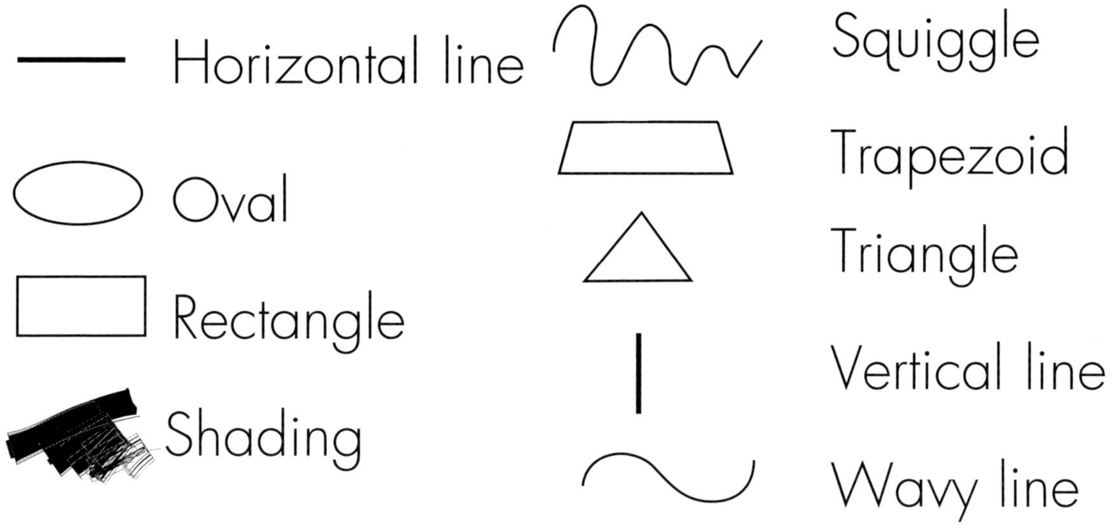

More About Russia

With 6,592,800 square miles (17,075,273.6 sq km) of land, Russia is the largest country in the world. It is twice the size of the United States! Russia lies across the northern parts of the continents of Europe and Asia. Russia has a population of 144 million people and is the sixth-most-populated country in the world. The majority of Russians are descendants of the eastern Slavs who founded Kievan Rus. About 4 percent of the population are Tartar, and 1.3 percent are Ukrainian. Moscow is the capital of Russia and its most-populated city, with 8,369,200 people. Founded in 1147, Moscow grew around the Kremlin, which means "fortress." The Kremlin was home to many of the Russian czars and is the seat of Russia's government today. Next to the Kremlin is Red Square, which has served as a public marketplace and as the site of ceremonies, demonstrations, and military parades.

St. Petersburg is Russia's second-largest city, with a population of 4,694,000. Located in northwest Russia near the country of Finland, St. Petersburg is the symbol of modern Russia and one of the most beautiful cities in

The Kremlin has been the political center of Russia since the late 1300s, when Dmitry Donskoy directed the building of its white stone walls and towers. From 1485 to 1495, the Kremlin was completely rebuilt, and it took on its present appearance and size at that time.

the world. When Peter the Great planned St. Petersburg, he modeled it after the great cities of western Europe. St. Petersburg was named in honor of Peter the Great's patron saint. When Lenin died of 1924, St. Petersburg was renamed Leningrad in honor of Lenin. In 1991, it took back its original name, St. Petersburg.

By owning the nation's farms, industries, and mines, the state controls Russia's economy. Products grown in Russia include grain, barley, fruits, wheat, vegetables, cattle, and hogs. Russia's main industries manufacture weapons, tractors, electrical equipment, and chemicals. The nation's mines produce iron ore, coal, diamonds, gold, lead, and salt. Russian is the national language of Russia and the common language of the 15 countries that belong to the CIS. In the tenth century, the grand prince of Kievan Rus became a Christian and made Christianity the state religion. During Communist rule, all religions were banned. Today, the Russian Orthodox Church is the official church of Russia. "Orthodox" means following church doctrines strictly.

Étienne-Maurice Falconet carved the *Bronze Horseman*, a statue of Peter the Great, shown here in a print from the 1800s, in St. Petersburg. Peter's horse steps on a snake, which represents the enemies of Peter and his reforms.

The Artist Vasily Polenov

Vasily Polenov (1844–1927) is considered one of Russia's most gifted landscape artists. Polenov was born in St. Petersburg. He studied art at the St. Petersburg Academy of Arts from 1863 to 1871. While Polenov was at the Academy, he won an

Vasily Polenov

important award called the Major Gold Medal for his painting *Raising of Jairus' Daughter*. He also won a trip to Paris, France, to study art. During his four years in Paris, Polenov was influenced by the French landscape artists from the Barbizon School. These artists painted outdoors, mostly near the village of Barbizon. They loved nature and painted landscapes just as they saw them. The Barbizon School artists used bright, clean colors and free-flowing brush strokes in their landscape paintings. Polenov was the first artist to introduce the Barbizon School techniques to Russia.

Polenov returned to Russia in 1876. He joined a group called the Wanderers. This group put on traveling art exhibitions. In 1878, Polenov exhibited his new, open-air style of painting by showing *Courtyard in Moscow*. This painting celebrates an everyday scene in Russia's capital. Polenov used rich colors and soft brush strokes to give the painting a lyrical quality. Lyrical art expresses harmony and the artist's feelings about his subject matter.

Polenov painted *Courtyard in Moscow* in 1878. It is done in oil on canvas and measures 23" x 32" (58.4 x 81.3 cm). At first glance, the painting could be a quiet backyard scene of an American home. However, when you look at the background, you notice the beautiful, tall, onion-domed buildings that are common in Moscow.

Map of Russia

Map of the Continent of Asia

Russia borders the Arctic Ocean in the north, the Pacific Ocean in the east, the Caspian and Black Seas in the south, and the Baltic Sea and eastern Europe in the west. Russia's highest peak is Mount Elbrus, which rises 18,510 feet (5,641.8 m) in the Caucasus Mountains on Russia's southern edge. Siberia, in the east, has some of the coldest weather on Earth. It is made up of ice-covered tundra in the north and taiga in the south. In eastern Siberia, Kamchatka Peninsula's frozen land, called the Land of Fire and Ice, is dotted with more than 100 volcanoes. The Lena River flows for 2,734 miles (4,399.9 km). It is Russia's longest river. Siberia's Lake Baikal is the world's deepest lake. It is about 5,315 feet (1,620 m) deep.

1

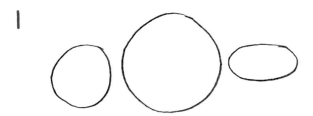

Draw your guides. They are a large circle in the center, a smaller circle to the left, and an oval to the right.

2

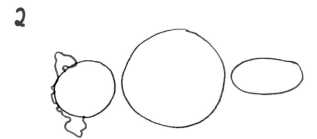

Draw wavy lines as indicated around the smaller circle.

3

Draw wavy lines, as shown, that attach the smaller circle to the larger circle.

4

Follow the wavy lines around the larger circle as shown.

5

Continue the wavy lines in and around the smaller oval and connecting again to the lines around the larger circle.

6

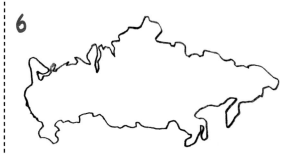

Erase the guides.

7

🪨	Central Siberian Plateau
◆	Lake Baikal
△	Mount Elbrus
●	St. Petersburg
☆	Moscow
▦	West Siberian Plain

Draw the small islands that surround Russia. Add symbols and a legend to show Russia's special places to visit.

Flag of Russia

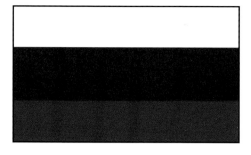

The Russian national flag was adopted by the order of President Boris Yeltsin on December 11, 1993. Peter the Great was the first to use this tricolor flag, which flew over Russia until 1917. Russia's national flag has three equal horizontal stripes. From top to bottom, the stripes are white, blue, and red. Although the colors have no official meaning, many Russians connect white with nobility, blue with honesty, and red with courage or love.

Currency of Russia

Russian currency consists of rubles. Soon after the USSR fell, the Russian government printed new money. However, they had no coat of arms. The government thought the old Russian coat of arms, the czarist two-headed eagle with three crowns, would be used without the crowns. They printed this on the back of the new currency. Parliament adopted this coat of arms but included the crowns, so now Russian currency has the incomplete coat of arms.

Flag

1

Draw a rectangle.

2

Add a horizontal line. It should be positioned about a third of the way down from the top.

3

Add another horizontal line, as shown.

4

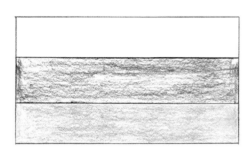

Shade the flag. The blue stripe in the center is darkest.

Currency

1

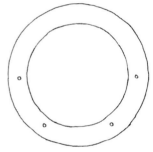

Draw two large circles and four very small circles on the right and the left sides.

2

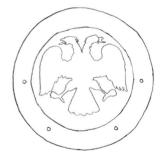

Draw the outline of the two-headed bird.

3

Draw the bird's feathers and eyes.

4

Draw in the Russian letters and numbers as indicated, and you're done!

Russia's Coat of Arms

Russia's coat of arms was adopted in 1993. It is similar to the emblem that stood for Russia from the fifteenth century until the 1917 revolution. The main design on the coat of arms is a gold eagle with

two heads. The eagle represents power and living forever. The two heads of the eagle stand for the European and Asian continents that Russia occupies. Three gold crowns are above the eagle. During the seventeenth century, the crowns stood for the union of three nations, Russia, Ukraine, and Belarus. Today they stand for the branches of the government. The eagle holds a scepter and a sphere in its claws to stand for the government's power. In the eagle's center there is a red shield with a white horse and a rider who wears a blue cape. These are the same colors that are on the national flag. The rider is stabbing a dragon with a spear. This is a symbol for the struggle between good and evil.

1 To begin drawing the coat of arms, draw a large rectangle.

2 Round off the bottom corners, and add a small point to the middle. Copy the shield shape in the center. Draw two circles to use as your guides as you complete the next steps.

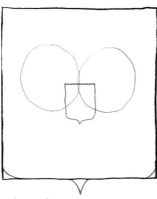

3 Begin by drawing three crowns. The crowns look like soft squares. They have a circle and a cross on top. Draw two flowing lines coming from the center crown.

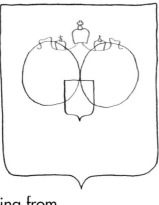

4 Under each of the smaller crowns, draw the profile of an eagle. Use a curving line to draw the sharp beak, chest feathers, and the top of the wing. Add a triangle below the center shield.

5 Add the feathers to each wing using U shapes. Draw curling tail feathers inside the triangle, using flowing J-shaped lines.

6 Draw the feathery top of each leg. Draw the back of each eagle's head. Some feathers are longer than other feathers.

7 Add the skinny bottom part of each leg. One leg holds a circle with a cross. The other leg holds a scepter. Draw the basic outline of a figure on a horse in the center of the shield. Erase extra lines.

8 Add details, and shade your drawing. Great work!

The Birch Tree

The sacred tree of Russia is the birch. It is prized by the people of Russia because it grows well in Russia's cooler climate and has many uses. The birch is found in the northern forests of Russia and even in Siberia. It grows from 40 to 80 feet (12.2–24.4 m) high and has bright green leaves that turn gold in autumn. The white bark of the birch tree is used to make shoes and baskets. In ancient times, the Slavs wrote letters and important documents on birch bark. They also made grease from the birch's tar and tea from its leaves. The wood of the birch tree provides fuel and is used to make utensils and beautiful furniture. One species, called the Karelian birch, exists only in Russia. Furniture and objects made from its wood are prized by people all over the world.

1 Draw a long, thin trunk. Notice the way it comes to a point at the top. Use a lumpy line because the bark has an irregular surface. The trunk of a tree carries food and water from the roots below the ground to the rest of the tree.

2 Add branches coming from the top half of the trunk. Branches hold the tree's leaves. Leaves produce food for the tree using light from the Sun.

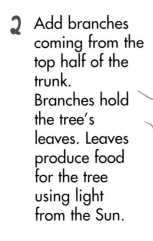

3 On the right side of the tree, add shorter branches coming from the longer ones.

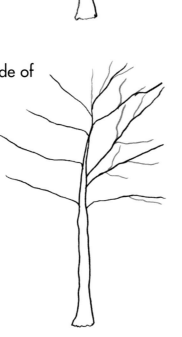

4 Repeat step 3 on the left side of the tree. Have fun with it!

5 Fill in the top of the tree with many small branches. Because this picture was taken in the winter, you do not have to add leaves.

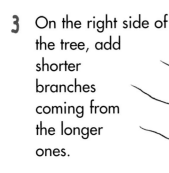

6 Shade your drawing. If you want, you can draw the tree as it might look in the spring. You could add leaves to your drawing.

21

St. Dimitrius Cathedral

St. Dimitrius Cathedral is located north of Moscow in Vladimir, which once served as Russia's capital. Vladimir is part of an area called the Golden Ring. This area got its name from the ring of small villages that have a rich collection of ancient stone churches and forts dating from the twelfth century. Some of the churches even have gold, onion-shaped domes!

Grand Prince Vsevolod III built St. Dimitrius to honor his patron saint and his son, Dmitri. Built between 1194 and 1197, St. Dimitrius is known for the beautiful carvings that decorate its outside walls. These stone images show Christian symbols, mythological characters, and ordinary things, such as an image of Vsevolod holding his newborn son.

1   This building is made using tall arches. Begin by drawing a tall, thin arch.

2   Add a larger arch next to the first arch.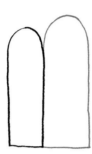

3   Add another arch. This one is a bit smaller.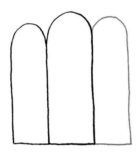

4   For the tower, draw a rounded square shape above the second and third arch. Draw a half circle on top for the dome.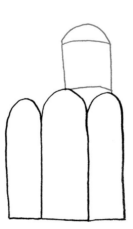

5   Draw a line connecting the top of each arch to its neighbor. Then draw a long hook shape on the right, which connects at the top and bottom to the last arch.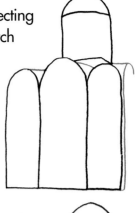

6   Draw an arched section coming out below the hook. Behind this shape, draw a similar section. Draw lines to form roofs. Add windows to the tower.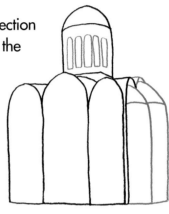

7   Add a decorative band of half circles to the dome. Add a vertical line to the top of the dome. Add hook-shaped lines inside each arch. Add three windows and a large, arching doorway.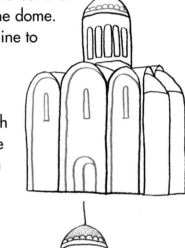

8   Shade your drawing. Notice the dark areas in each window and in the doorway.

St. Basil's Cathedral

Ivan the Terrible ordered St. Basil's Cathedral to be built in the heart of Moscow to commemorate Russia's defeat of the Mongols in 1552. Built between 1555 and 1561, the church was called the Cathedral of the Intercession of the Virgin. St. Basil's is named for a prophet who predicted the Moscow fire of 1547 and Ivan's murder of his own son. Basil the Blessed is buried under a chapel on the site.

St. Basil's Cathedral is special because it is made of eight pillarlike churches built on the same base around a larger church. Its unusual architecture includes many shapes, such as arches, towers, and onion-shaped domes. The cathedral is painted many different colors. According to legend, Ivan had the architect's eyes blinded so that he could never build another church like it.

1 Begin with five rectangles for the base of the cathedral. Notice their different shapes and sizes.

2 Add two bent lines from the first and last rectangle. On top of the center sections add triangles. Add a base for the triangle in the back to sit on.

3 Next begin stacking the shapes for the first tower. At the top is a beautiful shape called an 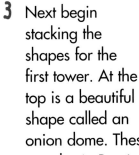 onion dome. These domes are very popular in Russia and other places in the world such as Turkey and Morocco.

4 Stack the shapes for the second tower. There should be four sections and an onion dome.

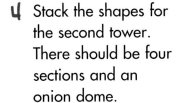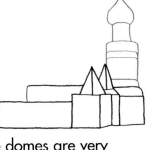

5 Stack the shapes for the third onion-domed tower. Then add the large tower in the back. Use curved and straight lines, triangular sections, and a small onion dome on top.

6 Add the three final onion-topped towers on the left. Notice the different shapes in each.

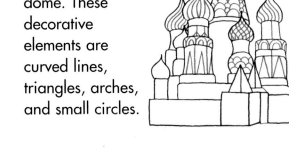

7 Add the beautiful decorative trimmings on each tower and dome. These decorative elements are curved lines, triangles, arches, and small circles.

8 Shade your cathedral. Add a tiny circle and a cross on top of each tower. Add details as shown.

25

Peter the Great

Peter the Great (1672–1725) was born in Moscow to the Russian ruler Alexis I and his second wife, Natalia. After Alexis died, Peter ruled alongside his half brother Ivan, with his half sister Sophia's guidance. In 1689, he took complete control and became the czar of Russia. During his reign, Peter visited European countries, where he learned naval warfare and shipbuilding. Peter also hired western experts, including doctors and engineers, to help modernize Russia. He even moved the capital from Moscow to the city of St. Petersburg so that he could be closer to Europe. Peter created a Russian navy, improved the army, introduced educational and church reforms, and opened Russia to western trade and culture. One of Russia's most beloved rulers, Peter is memorialized in the statue called the *Bronze Horseman* by Frenchman Étienne-Maurice Falconet.

1 Begin drawing the body of the horse with basic triangle shapes. These will be the guides for its head and front legs.

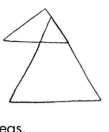

2 Add two diagonal lines to form guides for the horse's body. Draw straight lines to form the base on which the statue stands.

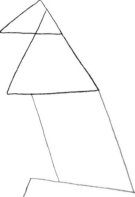

3 Begin drawing the horse's front legs. Use a curved line to shape each leg and the hooves.

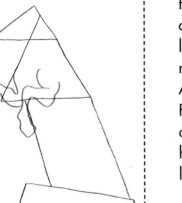

4 Draw the horse's head. Use the triangle guide to draw the lines of the nose, lips, and rounded jaw. Then draw the pointed ears and the zigzag of the mane. Connect the leg to the head.

5 Add the two rear legs using flowing lines. Then draw the simplified outline of Peter the Great. Peter's cape is a long shape that drops down the horse's back.

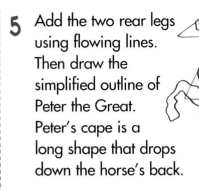

6 Next add Peter's arm and hand. Then add a vertical leg in two sections, and a rounded foot.

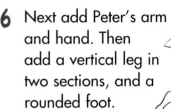

7 Add the arm and the foot on the other side of the horse. Draw a long, pointed sword near Peter's knee. Add the reins. Finally, add two curved lines to make the horse's tail. Erase extra lines.

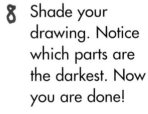

8 Shade your drawing. Notice which parts are the darkest. Now you are done!

The Winter Palace

In 1754, Catherine II, also known as Catherine the Great, hired Italian architect Bartolomeo Rastrelli to build a splendid palace in St. Petersburg. The palace was to be a winter home for the royal family. The Winter Palace's more than 400 rooms are decorated with rare woods, sculptures, and painted ceilings. The Winter Palace served as the royal family's winter residence for more than 100 years. During World War I, it was used as a hospital. Today, it is part of the Hermitage, one of the world's largest museums. The palace now houses about three million works of art that Peter I and Catherine II collected. Some of the collections include French tapestries, a silver-gilt English throne, and ancient artifacts.

1

Let's focus on the central area of the palace. It has the same elements as the rest of the palace, such as arches, columns, triangular pediments, and doorways. Start by drawing a slanted rectangle.

2

Add three lines across the building's facade. Facade is the word architects use for the face of the building.

3

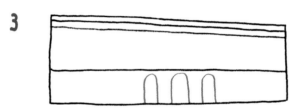

Add three arches. They are the entrance to the palace.

4

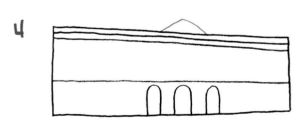

Add a triangle on top of the palace. This is called a pediment.

5

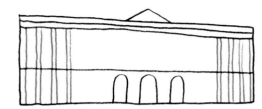

Draw seven vertical lines on each side of the building. These will make columns.

6

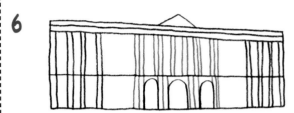

Add four clusters of double columns on the lower part of the building, next to the doors. Above the doors add four clusters of double columns and two single columns in the center.

7

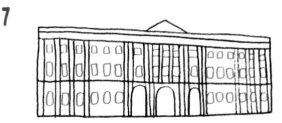

Draw 12 windows on the bottom level. Add 17 windows each on the middle and upper levels of the palace.

8

Add the pole and tiny figures to the top of the building. Shade your drawing.

Alexander Pushkin

Alexander Pushkin is considered Russia's greatest poet and the father of modern Russian literature. His works include short stories, poems, novels, and dramas. Pushkin is noted for writing about real events in Russian history. In several of his poems, Pushkin found fault with people in government. He was exiled twice. Pushkin was born into a noble family in Moscow in 1799. He studied at the Imperial School in the town of Tsarskoye Selo, which was renamed Pushkin in his honor. This statue is located in Pushkin. Pushkin was married to a beautiful woman named Natalya, who attracted many admirers. In 1837, Pushkin challenged one of these admirers to a duel and was killed.

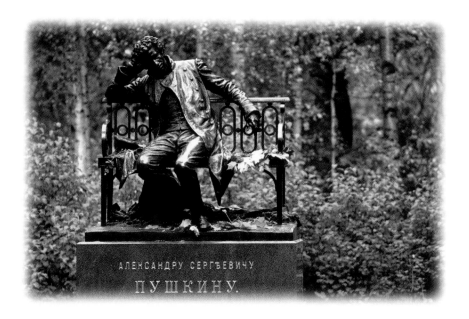

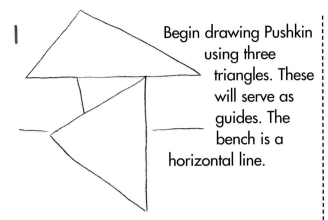

1 Begin drawing Pushkin using three triangles. These will serve as guides. The bench is a horizontal line.

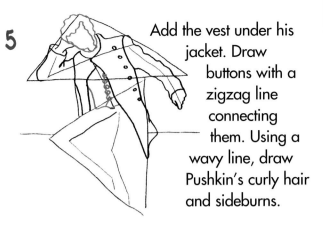

5 Add the vest under his jacket. Draw buttons with a zigzag line connecting them. Using a wavy line, draw Pushkin's curly hair and sideburns.

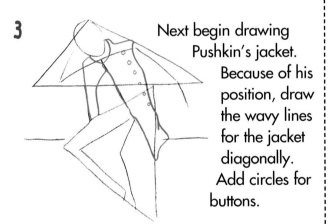

2 Inside the basic shapes sketch the stick figure version of Pushkin's body. Notice how one arm holds up his head and one drapes over the top of the bench.

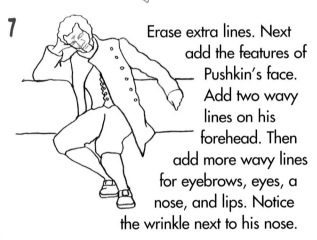

6 Next add the legs and the feet using soft wavy lines. Use the guide to help position the legs. His pants come to the knee. Add Pushkin's shoes with buckles.

3 Next begin drawing Pushkin's jacket. Because of his position, draw the wavy lines for the jacket diagonally. Add circles for buttons.

7 Erase extra lines. Next add the features of Pushkin's face. Add two wavy lines on his forehead. Then add more wavy lines for eyebrows, eyes, a nose, and lips. Notice the wrinkle next to his nose.

4 Use wavy lines to draw each sleeve. Draw the hand on the right using a triangular shape. Then add the hand on the left using two curved lines. The rest of the hand is behind the head.

8 Shade your drawing. Look for the darkest shadows and the lightest areas.

The Trans-Siberian Railway

Before the 1900s, transportation between western Russia and its eastern provinces was difficult. Horses were the only means of travel for long distances. Construction of the Trans-Siberian Railway began in 1891, and was completed in 1916. The railway, the world's longest, travels 5,778 miles (9,298.8 km) across the continent. Its last stop is Vladivostok in Siberia, pictured below. Most of the railroad workers were soldiers or exiled convicts in Siberia. Using axes, saws, shovels, and wheelbarrows, the workers built about 372 miles (598.7 km) of railway each day. Today the Trans-Siberian Railway is important to the Russian economy. It is the shortest route between Asia and Europe. The entire trip takes seven days!

1

Draw two rectangles and leave a large space between them.

2

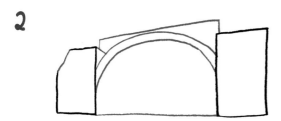

Erase the top left corner of the left rectangle. Add two arching lines that stretch like a rainbow between the rectangles. Above the arches draw the top of a square. Add the small diagonal line on the left connecting the corner of the left rectangle to the arch.

3

Stack six rectangular sections above the arch. Add the small section in the center that looks like an upside-down *U*.

4

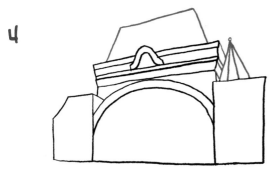

Add the large section to the top using diagonal lines. Add a triangle to the top of the right-hand rectangle. Divide the triangle into three sections.

5

Add four vertical lines on the rectangular section below the upside-down *U*. Under the arch add a band with two squares. Then add an entry with three arches.

6

Below each arch draw a post. Notice the different sections that make up each post. Add horizontal lines between each arch for stairs.

7

Draw the trimmings on the rectangular sections on each side of the building. The trimmings are made using lines and arches.

8

Shade your drawing. Notice where the darkest and lightest areas of the building are.

Fyodor Dostoyevsky

Fyodor Dostoyevsky (1821–1881) is one of Russia's greatest writers. The author was born in Moscow but spent most of his life in St. Petersburg. Dostoyevsky published his first novel, *Poor Folk*, in 1846. He used his personal experiences in his stories, and he often wrote about the poor or the oppressed. In 1849, he was sentenced to death for belonging to a group that discussed revolutionary ideas. Just before he was to be shot, Dostoyevsky was pardoned and sent to a Siberian prison for four years. Dostoyevsky used this experience to write two of his masterpieces, *The Idiot* and *The Brothers Karamazov*. Dostoyevsky died in

1881. He was buried in St. Petersburg's Tikhvin Cemetery. A bust of the author is at his tombstone.

1 Draw an oval outline for Dostoyevsky's head.

2 Add an outline of the chest. Then draw the diagonal lines to form the lapels of his jacket.

3 Begin drawing the outline of his face. Using a continuous line, draw, from the top down, the forehead, the curve of the eyebrow, the lump of the cheekbone, and the curve of the lower cheek, ending in the beard.

4 Next draw the high hairline and the shape of the patch of hair on the crown of his head.

5 Add the wavy shape of the hair on the right, the question-mark-shaped ear, and the fluffy beard and mustache.

6 Draw two curved eyebrows and two stern, almond-shaped eyes.

7 Add a diagonal line for the top of the nose, two rounded nostrils, and wrinkles around the eyes and on the forehead and cheeks.

8 Shade your drawing.

Vladimir Ilich Lenin

Vladimir Ilich Ulyanov (1870–1924) was born in the town of Simbirsk, today named Ulyanovsk. He adopted the name Lenin during his campaign for revolution. Lenin was influenced by Karl Marx's *Communist Manifesto* and other communist teachings. After he organized a workers' strike, Lenin was arrested and sent to Siberia. When he was released, Lenin moved to Europe and wrote for a newspaper that supported the overthrow of the government. After the Revolution of 1917, Lenin returned to Russia. He became the head of the Communist Party and, finally, the nation. Lenin started many socialist reforms, but he was a cruel leader. He forced Communism on the Russians and killed anyone who opposed him.

1

You will draw Lenin's tomb. A tomb is a building in which a dead body is placed. Start with a wide rectangle

2

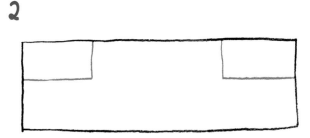

Add a rectangle in each of the top corners.

3

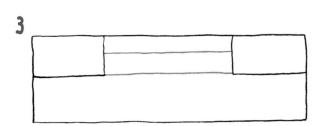

Draw two horizontal lines between the rectangles.

4

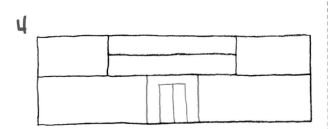

Add a double door. Draw a vertical line on each side.

5

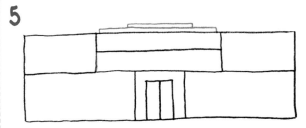

Draw two thin sections on top of the building.

6

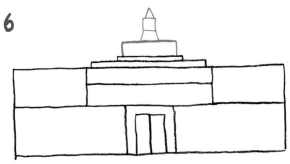

Draw four more sections. The first is a rectangle. The second section is a trapezoid, or rectangle with diagonal sides. The third is a square. The top is a triangle.

7

Add windows. Add the Russian letters over the door.

8

Shade your drawing.

Matryoshka Dolls

Painted wooden dolls that fit one inside the other are called matryoshka dolls. Matryoshka means "mother." Artists who wanted to preserve Russian folk art and peasant toys created the dolls in the 1890s. Folk art refers to art made by rural craftspeople who use materials and designs that reflect their communities.

The Russian matryoshka dolls are usually made from the wood of birch, aspen, or lime trees. The smallest doll, which is one piece, is made first. The next dolls are made in two pieces that fit together. Each of these dolls is made large enough to contain the smaller dolls that go inside it. After the dolls are shaped, they are painted in bright colors. Some matryoshka dolls show historical heroes, families, peasant girls, or characters from favorite books. The largest matryoshka had 72 pieces. It was made in 1970, in honor of Lenin's birthday.

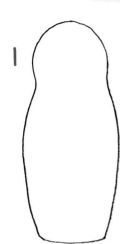

1 First outline the basic rounded shape of the doll.

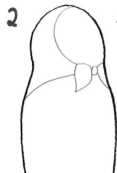

2 Add the curved lines of the scarf on her head. Draw the bow using teardrop shapes and a circle.

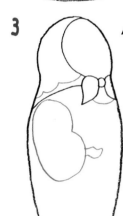

3 Add a ruffled line to the scarf. Add a puffy, rounded sleeve and a tiny hand. The hand bends because it will be holding fruit. Add an arc under the bow.

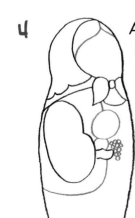

4 Add two curved lines for hair. Add another curved line for the doll's vest. Add fruit in her hand. The fruit can be made using two larger circles and then small circles clustered together for grapes.

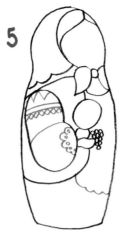

5 Add the trimmings on her sleeve. These can be made using V's, lines, X's, U's and circles. Then add a bumpy line at the bottom for her apron.

6 Add a flower to her scarf using teardrop-shaped petals. Add small teardrop shapes with curling tails below the doll's sleeve. Add flowers made with circles to the bottom of the apron. Add rounded shapes below the scarf.

7 Draw two arcs for her eyebrows, two almond-shaped eyes, two dots for her nostrils and a tiny mouth. The mouth can be made using a curvy line, like the top of a heart, for the top lip and a U for the bottom lip.

8 Shade your doll.

The Bank Bridge

St. Petersburg was built on more than 40 islands that were formed by the Neva River, its branches, and canals. More than 300 bridges cross the waterways to link the city together. One of the oldest bridges is the Bank Bridge. Built in 1825, it is a narrow suspension bridge that was built for pedestrians. On each end of the Bank Bridge stand two majestic griffins. A griffin is a mythological beast that has the body of a lion and the wings of an eagle. It stands for strength and the Sun. In some ancient myths, the griffin is the guardian of gold and other treasures. Russian sculptor Pavel Sokolov created the griffins out of cast iron. He accented their bronze-colored bodies with golden wings.

1 Begin by breaking the lion's body into two basic shapes. Use an upright oval for the front of the body and a diagonal oval for the rear.

2 Add the basic shape of the wing. It looks like a teardrop with one flat side.

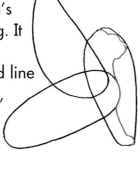

3 Begin by drawing the outline of the lion's face and front leg. It is made using a continuous curved line for the ear, brow, nose, mouth, chin, chest, leg, and paw.

4 Add another continuous curved line for the back of the leg, the chest, belly, rear leg, and back. Notice the way the leg folds under the lion like a Z or a 2.

5 Add a hook-shaped mark for the inner ear. Add the eye.

6 Next begin breaking the wing into its different feathered sections. Use bumpy lines. Erase extra lines.

7 Using curved lines draw feathers in the various sections of the wing.

8 Shade your griffin. Notice the dark area under the griffin's belly.

The Aurora

The Bolsheviks were revolutionaries who wanted to overthrow the government and replace it with

Lenin's Communist Party. Many of the Bolsheviks were peasants and factory workers. They wanted better working conditions and the same rights as the wealthy class. In 1917, the Bolsheviks organized trade unions, held demonstrations, and demanded that the large estates be split up among the peasants.

To achieve these reforms, the Bolsheviks started a revolution on October 25, 1917. It began when the battleship *Aurora* fired on the Winter Palace in St. Petersburg. It was a signal for the Bolsheviks to storm the palace. The Bolsheviks took control of the government overnight, and Lenin became the head of Russia. Built in 1900, the *Aurora* was sunk during World War II to keep it safe from the Germans. It was raised in 1944. Today the *Aurora* is a museum.

1

Draw a long rectangle that gets shorter on the right side. This is the basic shape of the body of the boat.

2

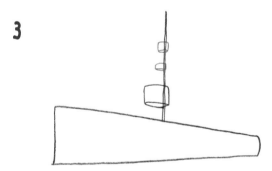

Add a tall pole and an observation deck attached to the pole. The observation deck is made using two vertical lines attached with rounded lines.

3

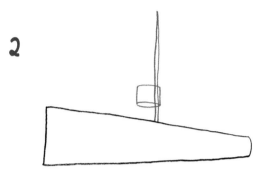

Add two more observation decks.

4

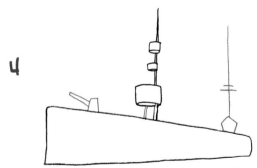

Draw the shape in the rear topped by a tall pole with two crosses. In the front of the boat, add a trapezoid with an arm coming out of it. Add another support under the lowest observation deck using two vertical lines.

5

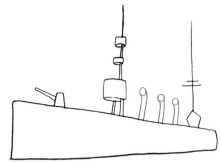

Add three tubes behind the observation decks. These are made using vertical lines that arch into circles at the top.

6

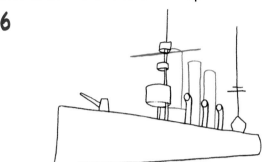

Draw three smoke stacks by the tubes. Add a horizontal line behind the observation deck. Add a large cross bar below the highest observation deck.

7

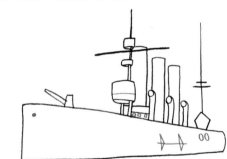

Add two circles on the side of the ship. Draw a horizontal line and add two triangles to it. Draw a tiny circle in the front of the boat.

8

Shade your ship. Great job!

Timeline

800s	Slavs establish the state of Kievan Rus, and the Vikings invade Russia.
900s	The grand prince of Kievan Rus accepts Christianity.
1240	The Mongols begin their 200-year rule of Russia.
1380	Ivan III gains Russia's independence from the Mongols.
1613	The 300-year Romanov dynasty begins.
1682–1725	Peter the Great reigns.
1703	St. Petersburg is founded by Peter the Great.
1762–1796	Catherine the Great reigns.
1812	Russia defeats Napoleon's armies.
1861	Alexander II abolishes serfdom.
1903	Lenin organizes the Communist Party.
1914	World War I begins.
1917	The last czar, Nicholas II, gives up the throne.
1917	The Bolshevik Revolution overthrows the provisional government.
1917–1924	Lenin is head of Russia and the Communist Party.
1929–1953	Stalin becomes dictator of Russia.
1939–1945	World War II is fought.
1945–1991	The cold war occurs.
1991	The former Soviet Union (USSR) is dissolved. The Commonwealth of Independent States (CIS) is formed.

Russia Fact List

Official Name	The Russian Federation
Area	6,592,800 square miles (17,075,273.6 sq km)
Population	144,417,000
Capital	Moscow
Most Populated City	Moscow, population 8,369,200
Industries	Weapons, electrical equipment, heavy machinery, chemicals
Agriculture	Grain, wheat, fruits, vegetables, cattle, hogs
Minerals	Iron ore, coal, lead, gold, diamonds, salt
Coat of Arms	Gold double-headed eagle
National Tree	Birch
National Animal	Brown bear
Highest Mountain Peak	Mount Elbrus, 18,510 feet (5,641.8 m)
Longest River	Lena River, 2,734 miles (4,399.9 km)
Language	Russian
National Holiday	June 12, Independence Day

Glossary

admirers (ad-MYR-urz) People who value someone or something a great deal.

architecture (AR-kih-tek-cher) The art of creating and making buildings.

artifacts (AR-tih-fakts) Objects created and produced by humans.

campaign (kam-PAYN) A plan to get a certain result.

civil war (SIH-vul WOR) A war between two sides within one country.

coat of arms (KOHT UV ARMZ) A picture on and around a shield.

commemorate (kuh-MEH-muh-rayt) To remember officially.

communism (KOM-yuh-nih-zem) A system in which the government owns all property and goods, which are shared equally by everyone.

convicts (KON-vikts) People who have been proven guilty of a crime.

culture (KUL-chur) The beliefs, practices, and arts of a group of people.

demonstrations (deh-mun-STRAY-shunz) Public displays for a person or a cause.

descendants (dih-SEN-dents) People born of a certain family or group.

doctrines (DOK-trinz) Things that are taught in a system of belief.

emblem (EM-blum) A picture with a saying on it.

engineers (en-jih-NEERZ) Masters at planning and building engines, machines, roads, bridges, and canals.

exhibitions (ek-sih-BIH-shuns) Public shows.

exiled (EG-zyld) Made to leave one's home or country.

experts (EK-sperts) People who know a lot about a subject.

horde (HORD) A huge group of people.

imperial (im-PEER-ee-ul) Having to do with an empire or an emperor

indigenous (in-DIH-jeh-nus) Having started in and coming naturally from a certain area.

influenced (IN-floo-ensd) To have produced an effect on others.

intercession (in-ter-SEH-shun) Prayer for another.

memorialized (meh-MOR-ee-uh-lyzd) Remembered in a special way.

mythological (mih-thuh-LAH-jih-kul) Made up in very old stories.

myths (MITHS) Stories that people make up to explain events.

nuclear (NOO-klee-ur) Having to do with the energy created by splitting atoms, the smallest bits of matter.

oppressed (uh-PRESD) Being kept down by use of power or authority.

parliament (PAR-lih-mint) The lawmakers of a country.

patron saint (PAY-trun SAYNT) A special saint who is thought to help an individual, a trade, a place, a group, or an activity.

pedestrians (puh-DES-tree-enz) People who are walking.

peninsula (peh-NIN-suh-luh) Land surrounded by water on three sides.

predicted (prih-DIKT-ed) Guessed based on facts or knowledge.

provinces (PRAH-vins-ez) The main parts of a country.

rebellions (ruh-BEL-yunz) Fights against one's government.

reformed (rih-FORMD) Changed or improved.

revolutionaries (reh-vuh-LOO-shuh-ner-eez) People who believe in ideas that go against what is commonly held to be true or correct.

revolutionary (reh-vuh-LOO-shuh-ner-ee) New or very different.

satellite (SA-til-yt) A spacecraft that circles Earth.

scepter (SEP-ter) A staff that a king or queen carries, a sign of power.

socialist (SOH-shuh-list) Having to do with a system in which there is no private property.

species (SPEE-sheez) A single kind of plant or animal.

sphere (SFEER) An object that is shaped like a ball.

suspension bridge (suh-SPEN-shun BRIJ) A type of bridge that is attached to land so as to hang down.

symbols (SIM-bulz) Objects or pictures that stand for something else.

taiga (TY-guh) Forests with fir and spruce trees that start where tundras end.

tapestries (TA-puh-streez) Fabrics with beautifully designed pictures sewn on them, used for curtains and hangings.

techniques (tek-NEEKS) Special methods or systems used to do something.

tundra (TUN-druh) A cold, treeless frozen plain.

utensils (yoo-TEN-sulz) Tools usually used in cooking or eating.

Index

Web Sites

Due to the changing nature of Internet links, PowerKids Press has developed an online list of Web sites related to the subject of this book. This site is updated regularly. Please use this link to access the list:
www.powerkidslinks.com/kgdc/russia/